"This book is written ... understanding of the Holy C ... shepherd and the flock migh ... _____ ...ent. It is a unique and timely book, for such a time as this."

Archbishop J. P. Hackman

President, TAPAC

UK

"Great is the unction in this book because great is the wisdom it unfolds. Rev indeed demonstrates throughout the pages that there is something supernatural about the bread we break and the cup we raise. You can never encounter the supernatural and remain the same."

Mr Francis Kingsley Codjoe

Country Controller, NCR Ghana Ltd

"This book is an insightful, thought provoking, readable piece of Christian literature...written by a true believer with a burning desire for the growth of Christians. Be blessed, encouraged and informed as you read."

Dr Lawrence Tetteh

President, Worldwide Miracle Outreach

UNDERSTANDING

The HOLY

COMMUNION

DANIEL GHANSAH

With a Foreword by Dr Lawrence Tetteh

UNDERSTANDING
The HOLY
COMMUNION

danielghansah.com

WestBow Press books may be ordered through booksellers or by contacting:

WestBow Press
A Division of Thomas Nelson
1663 Liberty Drive
Bloomington, IN 47403
www.westbowpress.com
1-(866) 928-1240

Because of the dynamic nature of the Internet, any web addresses or links contained in this book may have changed since publication and may no longer be valid. The views expressed in this work are solely those of the author and do not necessarily reflect the views of the publisher, and the publisher hereby disclaims any responsibility for them.

Any people depicted in stock imagery provided by Thinkstock are models, and such images are being used for illustrative purposes only.

Certain stock imagery © Thinkstock.

ISBN: 978-1-4497-9774-4 (sc)
ISBN: 978-1-4497-9775-1 (e)

Library of Congress Control Number: 2013910613

Printed in the United States of America.

WestBow Press rev. date: 6/12/2013

The author and publisher have taken reasonable precautions in the preparation of this book and believe the facts presented in the book are accurate as at the date it was written. However, neither the author nor the publisher assumes any responsibility for any errors or omissions. The author and publisher specifically disclaim any liability resulting from the use or application of the information contained in this book, and the information is not intended to serve as legal, financial or other professional advice related to individual situations.

Unless otherwise indicated, all Scripture quotations are from the *King James Version* and *New King James Version* of the Bible.

To My Wife and Children, and to All the Saints in Christ Jesus.

CONTENTS

FOREWORD BY
Dr Lawrence Tetteh

The Holy Communion is one of the most observed sacraments within Christendom. It is a key component of spiritual healing and reconciliation. The act of Holy Communion is also an expression of love and service to one another. This is also one sacrament in which sharing is inarguably clearly demonstrated.

The passion of the Church for this Holy Ordinance has been somewhat doused by the lack of in-depth literature about this all important sacrament. It is for these reasons that when Reverend Daniel Ghansah asked me to write the foreword for this book, *"Understanding the Holy Communion"* I obliged.

I have had a special relationship with Reverend Ghansah over the years and have a great deal of respect for his love and passion for the things of God. I greatly admire his humility in ministry and his consistent growth over the years. I have had the opportunity to minister in his church in Newcastle-Upon–Tyne and each time the experience was awesome.

His expertise and true professionalism are clearly exhibited in this book.

The book gives an in-depth but simplified view of the need to partake in Holy Communion. In Chapter 3 the book highlights the fact that this great sacrament is indeed a *Vehicle of Blessing*. The numerous benefits of the Holy Communion are enumerated in Chapter five of the book, underpinning the need for Christians to approach this sacrament with great faith.

On the question of how often one should partake in the Lord's Supper, the author cited the words of the Apostle Paul in his letter to the Corinthians Chapter 11 verse 25.... "do this as often as you drink it in remembrance of me....."

This book is an insightful, thought provoking, readable piece of Christian literature.

It is with great pleasure that I fully endorse this book written by a true believer with a burning desire for the growth of Christians.

Be blessed, encouraged and informed as you read *"Understanding the Holy Communion"*.

Dr Lawrence Tetteh
President, Worldwide Miracle Outreach
London, United Kingdom

Acknowledgement

My special thanks to my Senior Pastor, Mentor, Teacher and Guide, The Holy Spirit, for His inspiration.

A big thank you to the members of the Word of Faith Church Worldwide.

A special 'thank you' to Dr Lawrence Tetteh for taking time off your very busy schedule to read and write a foreword for this book. Knowing you is priceless. God bless you man of God.

To my Beloved Archbishop J P Hackman for your immense love, and for taking the time, to read through this work and to write about it. I sincerely do appreciate you.

Mr Francis Kingsley Codjoe, you've been with me all the way. Your love, care and endless support is second to none.

Appreciation is expressed to Dr Uzochukwu Cornelius Ugochukwu (PhD, MSc, BSc) and Pastor Mrs Irene Ghansah (MEd, PGCE, PgDip, BA Hons) for their immense help with the manuscript.

Finally, to my family for your unspeakable Love, Joy and Support. I Love You. *Kingdom Blessings*

9

PREAMBLE
(The Covenant Meal)

"And though these nobles of Israel gazed upon God, he did not destroy them. In fact, they ate a covenant meal, eating and drinking in his presence!

Exodus 24:11 NLT

"Then Jesus said unto them, Verily, Verily, I say unto you, Except ye eat the flesh of the Son of man, and drink his blood, ye have no life in you..."

John 6:53-58

Misconception in the body of Christ about the Holy Communion has robbed many of the fullness of the Blessing. As you can see from Exodus 24:11 above, there is a kind of eating and drinking in God's Presence which causes man to steer clear of destruction. When one opens the heart to eat at the Lord's Table as a response to God's calling in Revelation 3:20, which states "...if any man hear my voice and open the door, I will come in to him, and will sup with him, and he with

11

me", that individual has taken a giant step off the road of destruction and life plaques.

To partake of the Lord's Supper - eat of his body and drink of the 'cup' is to inject real life into your life. Destruction will be far away from you when you understand (discern) his body and by faith drink the cup. In the light of this, in the next few pages of this book, I'll be dealing with understanding the Holy Communion (its benefits, how to take it and how often you should take it).

However I will deal with *the value of understanding* in your walk with God first, before we go any further from there, because it's crucial.

Chapter 1

THE VALUE OF UNDERSTANDING

A good understanding of the ways of God will guarantee you a great standing in the race of life.

In the book of Proverbs we are advised to "tune our ears to wisdom, and concentrate on understanding." And it continues: "Cry out for insight and ask for understanding."

Proverbs 2:3-4 (NLT)

The NKJV states "apply your heart to understanding". (Proverbs 2:2). Therefore, there must be a deliberate effort from you if you want to walk in understanding. It is not something that will fall on you without your involvement. It says "apply your heart to understanding". The word "apply" in the Hebrew is to stretch forth or spread out. Which means to walk in understanding, you must stretch out for it. Before you can take hold of understanding, you are required to bend away from human traditions and elemental forces of the world. You must *stretch out* for understanding! And I must say that to walk in understanding is to actuate light, and when light is present, dominion over the affairs of life is inevitable.

According to Psalm 49:20, a person is no better than a beast if he/she lacks understanding. That's why God says He delights in people that show understanding.

"Thus says the Lord, Let not the wise man glory in his wisdom, neither let the mighty man glory in his might, let not the rich man glory in his riches: But let him who glories glory in this, <u>that he understands</u> and knows me, that I am the Lord which exercise loving-kindness, judgment, and righteousness, in the earth: for in these things I delight, says the Lord."

Jeremiah 9:23-24

In 1 Corinthians 11:29-30, the Bible gives <u>one</u> reason for weakness, sickness and untimely death among God's people and that reason is: lack of *discerning* the Lord's body, or put it this way: "not *discerning* the Lord's body." We will come back to this word *discerning,* but the truth is when we understand the power and place of the Holy Communion in our lives we will walk in better health, and this is what the Lord delights in. The struggles will be over, infirmities blown away, diseases healed, depression conquered and divine health becomes our birth right.

Do you know that "a man that wanders out of the way of understanding shall remain in the congregation of the death"? Proverbs 21:16. There is always 'death' when you wander out of the way of understanding. But that shall not be your portion in the name of Jesus Christ. Your portion is to have a meal in His presence where "none of those diseases" will come upon you (See Deuteronomy. 7:15).

Beloved, when you show understanding you are demonstrating respect and that respect for the Holy Communion is what releases the Spirit of Grace on you.

Look at this:

"Of how much sorer punishment, suppose ye, shall he be thought worthy, who hath trodden underfoot the Son of God, and hath counted the blood of the covenant, wherewith he was sanctified, an unholy thing, and hath done despite unto the Spirit of grace?"

Hebrews 10:29

Thus despising the Holy Communion, treating it like an invaluable thing in your life, is a *direct* disregard and disrespect to the Holy Spirit. You honour the Father by honouring the Blood of Jesus. This is very important. There is a scripture I want us to consider and it says:

"...Sanctify yourselves against tomorrow, and ye shall eat flesh: for you have wept in the ears of the Lord, saying, who shall give us flesh to eat? For it was well with us in Egypt: therefore the Lord will give you flesh and you shall eat. You shall not eat one day, nor two days, nor five days, neither ten days, nor twenty days; But even a whole month, until it come out at your nostrils, and it be loathsome unto you: **because that you have despised the Lord which is among you,** and have wept before him, saying, Why came we forth out of Egypt?"   Numbers 11:18-20

The word **despised** there is to **spurn** or **reject**. It also means to **disappear** or **cast away**. It therefore drops a hint that people can cause the presence of God among them to disappear. Here, I don't mean God will leave you, but his miracle working power is hindered. The truth is you can melt away or desecrate divine presence around you, which is what happens when you look down on the Lord's Supper. Do not show any contempt by taking communion anyhow. Do not turn down God's offer of life and wholeness for you by neglecting to walk in an understanding of this, rather honour and embrace the Lord by partaking of the Holy Communion in Understanding and Faith.

There is a Spirit called the Spirit of grace among us, and when you despise the blood of Jesus by not understanding the Holy Communion you scorn His manifestations in your life.

Over the years, I've seen people take the Holy Communion anyhow (which is purely due to lack of understanding) and due to this they have failed to live healthy lives. And I have also witnessed people under my ministry, experience strange healing and divine manifestations by applying themselves to the power of the Holy Communion.

A woman diagnosed of hepatitis B, who couldn't further her medical profession because of this problem, received complete healing by taking the Holy Communion. Some have escaped the threat of the enemy at the labour ward through this.

On the other hand, there is also the misconception preached by many that if one has committed any offence, or sin before going to church, then that individual is not 'qualified' to partake of the Holy Communion. Now, I find that strange because I cannot pick any man on earth without offence. In fact, when one has been overpowered by sin and plagued by guilt, that's when the person should be encouraged to boost his standing power through the Blood of the Lamb for we overcome (including sin and all habitual weakness etc.) by the Blood of the Lamb. I'm not advocating that people continue in sin, however, I do believe through the teachings of the Word of God that a person can overcome any habitual or sin related issues by understanding the place of the Blood of the Lamb of God.

You see, there is a difference between a Christian who has sinned and the sinner who doesn't know the Lord. The Christian who has been overcome by sin should be made to understand the power of the blood, instead of raining guilt on the person.

Teach the person to come boldly before the communion table and settle any difference. Encourage that individual to run to the Throne of Grace to receive help in times of need. Help him to receive his deliverance from the Lord and stand strong. James in his letter advised that "my brothers and sisters, if one of you wanders from the truth, someone can bring that person back." And I want to say, you should be the one to help people find the truth. Don't push them away with any religious holier-than-thou attitude. It's so sad that some churches will not even allow a person who is not a member of their congregation to take communion in that church as if they own the Lord's Supper. When the Bible says "we, being many, are one body in Christ..." Romans 12:5. And all this is because of lack of understanding.

There is so much misconception about the Holy Communion just as in the area of faith. But, let's take a journey in this project to discover our rights.

Looking at 1 Corinthians 11:28-30, we gain insight into the place of the Lord's Supper in our lives.
"But let a man examine himself, and so let him eat of that bread, and drink of that cup. For he that eateth and drinketh <u>unworthily</u>, eateth and drinketh

damnation to himself, not discerning the Lord's body. For this cause many are weak and sickly among you, and many sleep."

The word '*discern*' means: To perceive, recognise, to make out, to judge, to separate thoroughly or understand. We have failed to knock out weaknesses and sicknesses from our camp simply because we have failed in discerning the Lord's body.

We have failed to discern that Jesus Christ brought us into an irrevocable covenant with the Most High God, which guarantees our wholeness when He (Jesus) went to the Cross. This is the covenant which has the signature of the Most High God, and God wants us to discern that - thoroughly separating this (Holy Communion) from any other meals we are used to on this earth. This covenant, which is the binding agreement between heaven and earth, is what secured our wholeness. It is the *binding of the nature and form of God and the nature and form of man.* Therefore, the Holy Communion is a way of bringing together two forms -

the Form of God and the form of man. One is Supernatural and the other is natural. One is the Strongest and the other is the weakest. It is the coming together of the Nature of God and the nature of Man. At the communion hour, there is interflow of a certain "DNA", and this must be accepted by you for the power to be released.

It must be settled in your heart that there is never a Communion time that God is missing! Anytime Holy Communion is taken, God comes to the table to ensure the fulfilment of His Word. It's a covenant He has made and "civilisation" cannot annul His Faithfulness. Oh that the eyes of our understanding maybe opened! Sadly, we are the ones who stand to suffer if we fail to discern the body. Our lack of faith or belief does not change the ordinance of God. Paul said "For this cause many are weak and sickly among you, and many sleep (dead)".

Understand this: partaking of the Holy Communion has great significance in your life. And anytime you take the Holy Communion, you exalt His Word over anything in your life. You put the Law of the Spirit of Life in Christ to work in you.

Do you remember the gathering and eating of manna had to be done according to divine instructions and it was that food (manna) which was responsible for the unusual physical strength the people of God had in the wilderness (as stated in the scriptures). That manna was a vehicle of blessing! The scriptures say there was no feeble one among them. (See Psalm 105:37). Well, if there was no feeble one among them, then we can also get to the place where "there will be no feeble one among us. Our camp shall be a healthy, strong and joyous one" and this is going to be the benefit of this divine institution (The Holy Communion).

However, for this to become our experience we have to walk in understanding and the partaking of communion practiced within the law of faith. Did you ever read of anyone weak among the early Christians in the book of Acts? No, because "they continued steadfastly in breaking of bread" (Acts 2:42). In fact, Acts 20:7

records "the disciples came together to break bread on the first day of the week". They purposefully gathered to break bread. It was the breaking of bread for which they gathered. These disciples relentlessly kept the Lord's Supper so the Lord also kept them strong and healthy for His work.

If you know that the Holy Communion is a divine commission and institution, you will obey it. It's vital we discern the body. It is imperative we take communion in faith.

Chapter 2

THIS IS FOR LIFE

When it comes to the Communion, Paul says it takes the wise.

"I speak as to wise men; judge what I say. The cup of Blessing which we bless, is it not the Communion of the blood of Christ? The bread which we break, is it not the communion of the body of Christ?"

1 Corinthians 10:15-16

Every wise person in the kingdom of God knows the place of the communion in this life, because the wise will not allow the devil to rob them of God's Blessing, knowing that the Communion of the blood of Christ is called the cup of Blessing and *it is so for a reason.*

In the scriptures, there are different cups mentioned. There is a cup of suffering in Mark 10:38; there is the cup of judgement in Jeremiah 49:12; there is the cup of consolation in Jeremiah 16:7 and there is the cup of devils in 1 Corinthians 10:21. Moreover, there is a cup that causes curse in Numbers 5. But there is also The Cup of the Lord, (1 Corinthians 10:21), and each of these have their specific meanings and feats, but the Cup of the Lord which is the Cup of Blessing is what causes certain specific Blessings to **swell** in the life of the believer.

Heaven instituted the Holy Communion as the cup of blessing for mankind. It is a cup that can influence your very own nature, for it carries within it the very nature of God. The life of God is in it because the life of the flesh is in the blood (Leviticus 17:11). It is therefore necessary that anytime you partake of the communion, you ask the Father what you want "this Blessing" to do in your life. In fact, the Amplified Bible says in 1 Corinthians 10:16 that it is upon the cup of blessing [of wine at the Lord's Supper] that we ask [God's] blessing," It is written in Isaiah "Produce your cause...put me in remembrance: let us plead together:" (Isaiah 41:21&43:26); and the assurance in Zechariah is "as for thee also, by the blood of thy covenant I have sent forth thy prisoners out." (Zechariah 9:11). We have a stronger plea because of the covenant blood of Jesus. Maybe you want deliverance from certain habitual difficulty or you want healing in your body or to overcome the adversary. Whatever it is, the plea is stronger because of the Blood.

Looking at John 6:50-60 from the Holman Christian Standard Bible (HCSB), we find some immortal words from the lips of the Master about the Holy Communion:

"This is the bread that comes down from heaven so that anyone may eat of it and not die. I am the living bread that came down from heaven. If anyone eats of this bread he will live forever. The bread that I will give for the life of the world is My flesh.

At that, the Jews argued among themselves, 'How can this man give us His flesh to eat?'

So Jesus said to them, 'I assure you: Unless you eat the flesh of the Son of Man and drink His blood, you do not have life in yourselves. Anyone who eats My flesh and drinks My blood has eternal life, and I will raise him up on the last day, because My flesh is real food and My blood is real drink. The one who eats My flesh and drinks My blood lives in Me, and I in him. Just as the living Father sent Me and I live because of the Father, so the one who feeds on Me will live because of Me. This is the bread that came down from heaven; it is not like the manna your fathers ate - and they died. The one who eats this bread will live forever. He said these things while teaching in the synagogue in Capernaum. Therefore, when many of His disciples heard this, they said, **"This teaching is hard! Who can accept it?"**

You see, most people have not fully come to the understanding of the Communion. Even the disciples said, "This teaching is hard! Who can accept it?" And the situation is the same in our days. When it comes to truly partaking of the Holy Communion, not for religious reasons but for life purposes - the very intent for which it was established, it becomes hard for many. It is not difficult to take for religious reasons though, as a religious practice - yes, but for healing and wholeness - No! However, we have no problem taking an oval shaped starchy stuff given to us which we are told, as antibiotics, is able to fight virus but we do struggle to switch this same faith that we have towards the Lord's body.

The bread we break is the Communion of the body of Christ and is for Life. It is not a ritual, but for healing. It is a healing meal! It is the pot of the Lord to terminate any poison in your blood and body. It carries the force of heaven to flush out any toxic substance in your system. If you believe it, the power in it will go to work in you. That is when you will know and understand the immeasurable and unlimited and surpassing greatness of His power in and for us who believe as stated in Ephesians. (See Ephesians 1:19 AMP). This works when faith is put to work. The communion is divine life in the form of a physical substance to infuse life. When you take communion, any element of death in your life comes to an end. Just as Jesus' earthly journey ended on the cross, so does communion end any journey of darkness in your life. Therefore, turn on the light and dispel any darkness in your life by engaging the power of the bread and the cup.

If we take a step back into the Old Testament, we will discover amazing scriptural insight. And if the New Testament (Covenant) is better than the Old Testament (Covenant), then we must expect more infallible proofs from the Lord in the practice of His Truth.

From 2 Kings 4:38-41, we read:

"And Elisha came again to Gilgal: and there was a dearth (famine) in the land; and the sons of the prophets were sitting before him: and he said unto his servant, Set on the great pot, and seethe pottage for the sons of the prophets. And one went out into the field to gather herbs, and found a wild vine, and gathered thereof wild gourds his lap full, and came and shred them into the pot of pottage: for they knew them not. So they poured out for the men to eat. And it came to pass, as they were eating of the pottage, that they cried out, and said, O thou man of God, there is death in the pot. And they could not eat thereof. But he (Elisha) said, Then bring meal. And he (Elisha) cast it into the pot; and he said, Pour out for the people, that they may eat. **And there was no harm in the pot.**"

And there was no harm in the pot. So, after the introduction of the 'meal' by Elisha into the pot, there was no harm found again in the pot. What a miracle! If we knew who we are and by faith introduce the meal of God (communion) into our body, we will also find out that every toxic, disease breeding agents and infections no longer have any hold in our bodies. We will (by the power of the bread and the cup) terminate any death threatening hold in our life. For if we are all partakers of that one bread, (1 Cor. 10:17), then we must all enjoy that common health. If Paul was strong because he was a partaker of that bread, then we must be strong and well. If feebleness left the Israelites because they ate manna, we should expect even more. For if the ministry of condemnation had glory, the ministry of righteousness overflows with even more glory. So expect more from God in your walk with Him.

Chapter 3

VEHICLES OF BLESSINGS

Let's look at a scenario where one visits a General Practitioner (GP) with a certain disorder in the body. After examination by the GP, the GP prescribes a certain antibiotic for that individual to take. Well, that drug is the GP's way of helping, isn't it? It's the GP's vehicle of administering 'order' in the body and that individual (the patient) will have to cooperate with the GP by taking those medications to stand any chance of seeing desired result. The situation is similar in your walk with God.

According to the teachings of the Holy Scriptures, there is what I call vehicles of divine blessing. These are avenues appointed by God to cause healing grace to manifest in His children. There are certain "instruments" clearly defined in the Bible chosen by God to minister divine blessing to His people. And these do not place any limitations on Kingdom Blessings but they certainly have their place in God's manifestations in man's journey on earth. In the natural, there are vegetables from which we get our large selection of Vitamins A, K, B6 and so on; then also are the fruits such as oranges (which contain vitamin C, potassium as well as antioxidant) or pea, which give very important nutrient to our body. These things (foods) were made by God but they don't limit God in your life. Taking oranges doesn't mean you have no faith, rather it shows you have enough sense to use what your Father has made available for your benefits. Some people think that using the anointing oil means you don't have enough faith in God, or you're not being spiritual 'enough' but the Bible encourages the use of the anointing oil.

"Is anyone among you sick? Let him call for the elders of the church, and let them pray over him anointing him with oil in the name of the Lord" (From James 5:14). Why did handkerchiefs and aprons from Paul's body bring healing to the people? Why did Elisha cast meal into the pot to bring healing? Why should Elders anoint the sick with oil in the name of the Lord to bring healing? The truth is, the wisdom behind these belongs to the Lord. Nobody counsels the Most High. In His wisdom, He has approved certain avenues or vehicles whereby the believer can easily connect with the supernatural.

God used Peter's shadow to heal the sick and so on. "Insomuch that they brought forth the sick into the streets, and laid them on beds and couches, that at least the shadow of Peter passing by might overshadow some of them. There came also multitude out of the cities round about unto Jerusalem, bringing sick folks, and them which were vexed with unclean spirits: and they were healed everyone." (Acts 5:15-16).

Therefore, God can use anything. The following are some identified avenues used by God in the past, to prophetically bring to our attention the efficacy of the Holy Communion.

THE POT OF THE LORD

Let's go back to 2 Kings 4:38-41 again and look at something of great interest.

"And Elisha came again to Gilgal: and there was a dearth in the land; and the sons of the prophets were sitting before him: and he said unto his servant, Set on the great pot, and seethe pottage for the sons of the prophets. And one went out into the field to gather herbs, and found a wild vine, and gathered thereof wild gourds his lap full, and came and shred them into the pot of pottage: for they knew them not. So they poured out for the men to eat. And it came to pass, as they were eating of the pottage, that they cried out, and said, O thou man of God, there is death in the pot. And they could not eat thereof. But he said, Then *bring meal*. And he cast it into the pot; and he said, Pour out for the people, that they may eat. And there was no harm in the pot."

Here, the 'Meal' was the instrument of healing used in curing any harm found in the pot. It was a vehicle -

carrying God's healing power used by the prophet of God to deal with the threat of the devil in the pot.

In Proverbs 9:1-5; Wisdom says there is a meal prepared for us to partake of and walk in an uncommon wisdom. "Come eat of my bread, and drink of the wine which I have mingled." verse 5. So there is a prepared meal! There is a table set for you to silence your enemies. There is a meal, divinely made to neutralise any harm in your life. From this meal, you shall be immunised with divine life against any deadly pestilence.

The Holy Communion is God's meal to cure any poison in your 'pot'. All you need to do is to cast the Meal (the blood and the body) into your system and see if there will be any more harm in your life. There is no need to be religious about it! Just as Elisha cast that meal into the pot, and it cured every harm, even much more would partaking in the meal of the Lord execute greater effect on our lives. All impairment, evil and satanic reign will be swallowed up!

I expect miracles in partaking of the Communion. Is there any death in your life? Are you facing any threat? Then come before the Lord, lift the Cup and claim your freedom. For this reason the Son of God was manifested that he might destroy the works of the devil. You see, your deliverance was taken care of in the covenant of the Lord. And since a covenant mostly ends in a feast (See Genesis 31:43-54 and Exodus 24:9-11), you regularly partake in the Holy Communion to affirm to all parties around (visible or invisible) that you have a covenant of peace with the Most High God, sealed by the Blood of Jesus, and that your redemption is secured in His blood.

THE WATER THAT CAUSES CURSE AND THE BLOOD THAT CAUSES BLESSING

In Numbers 5:11-22 is found another powerful example of divine instrumentality.

"And the Lord spoke to Moses, saying, Speak to the children of Israel, and say to them, If any man's wife go aside, and commit a trespass against him, And a man lie with her carnally, and it be hidden from the eyes of her husband, and be kept close, and she be defiled, and there be no witness against her, neither she be taken with the manner; And the spirit of jealousy come upon him, and he be jealous of his wife, and she be defiled: or if the spirit of jealousy come upon him, and he be jealous of his wife, and she be not defiled: Then shall the man bring his wife unto the priest, and he shall bring her offering for her, the tenth part of an ephah of barley meal; he shall pour no oil upon it, nor put frankincense thereon; for it is an offering of jealousy, an offering of memorial, bringing iniquity to remembrance. And the priest shall bring her near, and set her before the Lord: And the priest shall take <u>holy water</u> in an earthen vessel; and of the dust that is in the floor of the tabernacle the priest shall take, and put it into the water: And the priest shall set the woman before the Lord, and uncover the woman's head, and put the offering of memorial in her hands, which is the jealousy offering: *and the priest shall have in his hand the bitter water that causes the curse.* And the priest shall charge her by an oath, and say unto the woman, If no man have lain with thee, and if thou hast not gone aside to uncleanness with another instead of thy husband, be thou free from this bitter water that causes the curse: But if thou hast gone aside to another instead of thy husband, and if thou be defiled, and some man have lain with thee beside thine husband: Then the priest shall charge the woman with an oath of cursing, and the priest shall say unto the woman, The Lord make thee a curse and an oath among thy people, when the Lord doth make thy thigh to rot, and thy belly to swell; **And this water that causes (brings) the curse shall go into thy bowels, to make thy belly to swell, and thy thigh to rot:** And the woman shall say, Amen, amen." Strange!

In the above scripture, you will find a peculiar instruction from the Lord to help the priest execute his office without any struggles. In matters so difficult to tell in those days, God gave instructions to help dissolve any doubts and this was one of them. Looking at verse 21; the scriptures say that the thigh would rot and the belly would swell if the woman in question was guilty of the accusation brought before the priest. But the next verse categorically states how this supernatural feat was to be brought about.

Verse 22 "And this water that causes or brings the curse shall go into thy bowels, to make thy belly to swell, and thy thigh to rot:"

It appears to me that after the Priest had taken ordinary water and prayed over it, that water took on a different form which was able to cause something to happen - a curse. The scriptures state, **this water that causes the curse**. Water, that is capable of causing distortions in the human body? Think about that. Water! I mean water. How much more shall the blood of Christ, who through the eternal Spirit offered himself without spot to God, purge your conscience from dead works to serve the living God? (Hebrews 9:14). We have something stronger which causes the Blessing not curse. We have the Blood that causes order in our body; that travels down the soul to purge the conscience. We have the Blood that speaks better things. This Blood empowers us to rule and reign in life. This is the Blood that causes the Blessing to SWELL in your life. So take it in Faith, in honour and in reverence and expect a miracle.

MANTLES

The woman with the issue of blood touched the hem of Jesus' garment and the virtue of God permeated into the woman's body to cure her of that evil that had plagued her life for years. Mark 5:25-34.

Was it the garment that healed the woman? No! Big No!!! For Jesus said in verse 34 " ...Daughter, thy faith hath made you whole; go in peace, and be whole of your plague." It was her faith. You see, her faith was seeking for a point of contact with the Master. There is something called faith connection. There are certain people and atmosphere that help you to release your faith quicker and stronger. As iron sharpens iron; so a man sharpens the countenance of his friend. That woman's faith was a seeking one. Sometimes, all that you need is to find something to connect with and your voice will be active. Her faith initiated the whole process in verse 27 when she touched the garment of the Master. By that act, the woman's faith communicated to Jesus, and Jesus replied, "Who touched my clothes?" in verse 30.   Never be caught in the trap of underestimating the mystery of divine vehicles.

I have had someone come to lie down on my bed and instantly received healing. One person bought me handkerchiefs to use on myself; and be given back to her after I have used them. When she used them, God supernaturally visited her and cured her of ailments. In one of late R.W. Schambach's meetings, a blind woman went forward and asked this dear man of God to spit into her eyes and she would be healed. Initially, the man of God hesitated but later gave in. Now it happened that, as soon as he spat on this woman's eyes, she received her sight. Friend, it can happen again. Some have received their healing by a man of God placing his hands on them, so listen to the voice of your faith. There is something within us that helps to connect better when we have a point of contact. This is Scriptural! If God honoured handkerchiefs and aprons from Paul's body to heal the sick in the early days of the New Testament, I don't see why God will not honour it again? God will do it again and again! For Jesus is the same yesterday, today and forever.

"And God wrought special miracles by the hands of Paul. So that from his body were brought unto the sick handkerchiefs or aprons, and the disciples departed from them, and the evil spirits went out of them."

Acts 19:11-12

Elisha used the mantle that came off Elijah to part river Jordan.

"He took up also the mantle of Elijah that fell from him, and went back and stood by the bank of Jordan; ... and said where is the LORD God of Elijah? and when he also had smitten the waters, they parted hither and thither: and Elisha went over."

2 Kings 2:13-14

By picking up the mantle, it was as though Elijah was still there. He (Elisha) identified with His Master (Elijah), even though the master was not there. Elisha remembered Elijah. Apostle Paul said "those things, which you have both learned, and received, and heard, and seen in me, do; and the God of peace shall be with you." Do those 'things' and the peace of God shall manifest. And Jesus said, do this in Remembrance of Me. Do you want to remember the Lord? Do you want the peace of God? Then lift up the Cup of Blessing and judge any situation which contradicts the Word of God. Execute the written judgement of God by coming before the table of the Lord and command the will of God in your life by partaking of the communion. Remember what the Lord of lords did for you. Lift up the Cup and the Bread and boldly declare that you are redeemed from the curse and that the Blessing of Abraham is working in your life.

These points of contact have their place in our conscious mind as far as divine manifestations are concerned. Some blessings in your life only become active after taking the Holy Communion. Physical things that have God's Instruction attached to them do matter to God, in that you carry a physical body created by God. Your healing and wellbeing matter to God. Why should Adam be banished from the garden after eating that fruit? It is the divine instruction released and connected to it that makes the difference. Jesus said "this do in remembrance of me."

Look at another vehicle used by Elisha to manifest the supernatural. And one of the things we must be aware of is that, in the use of these instruments it is extremely important we hold in addition the place of declaration. This declaration is the affirmation of your conviction. The woman with the issue of blood said within her before touching the avenue. In the case of Elisha, you will witness the *combination* of declaration and instrument as in many cases. Make a declaration anytime you hold the bread and the cup of blessing.

In the following scripture we see Elisha cured water and land by using natural things.

"And the men of the city said unto Elisha, Behold, I pray thee, the situation of this city is pleasant, as my lord sees: but the water is naught (bad), and the ground barren. And he said, 'Bring me a new cruse (bowl), and put salt therein.' And they brought it to him. And he went forth unto the spring (source) of the waters, and cast the salt in there, and said, '*Thus says the Lord, I have healed these waters; there shall not be from thence any more death or barrenness.*' So the waters were healed unto this day, according to the saying of Elisha which he spoke".

2 Kings 2:19-22

When you 'cast' the bread into your system, declare the Word of the Lord also over your life - 'Thus says the Lord, "I have healed you", there shall be no death or barrenness in my life. The numbers of my days shall be fulfilled. All that is mine come to me and I'm filled with the fullness of God in the Name of Jesus'. In this, you experience the combined EFFECT of His Blood and

Body (The Holy Communion) in your life! No matter how bad the issue might be, God can heal it.

THE LAYING ON OF HANDS

"They shall take up serpents; and if they drink any deadly thing, it shall not hurt them; *they shall lay hands on the sick, and they shall recover.*"

Mark 16:18

You are 'wired' to the supernatural! Our hands are a medium. The hands are one of God's chosen avenues to display his power through us and it is an earthen vessel. A chosen channel for the transfer of power. He says 'lay your hands on the sick and they shall recover'.

The laying on of hands is more of a spiritual act than physical. Of course the physical side is the visible contact of body but what goes on spiritually is more than what any human mind can grasp. There is a transfer of power in the laying on of hands. Something happens in the hand-laying event. I always advise people to be careful of who is laying hands on them, because transfer seems to happen anytime hands are laid.

"And the Lord said unto Moses, Take thee Joshua the son of Nun, a man in whom is the spirit, and lay thine hand upon him; And set him before Eleazar the priest, and before all the congregation; and give him a charge in their sight. And thou shalt put some of thine honour upon him, that all the congregation of the children of Israel may be obedient."

Numbers 27:18-20

So laying of hands is a divine institution.

Again, there is clear demonstration from the above scripture that Moses was to put honour on Joshua through laying on of Hands. When hands are laid, something of the person laying hands comes on the one whom hands are laid. There is a transfer.

And it is written: **"And Joshua the son of Nun was full of the spirit of wisdom; for Moses had laid his hands upon him: and the children of Israel**

hearkened unto him, and did as the Lord commanded Moses." Deuteronomy 34:9

That is impartation! And the dead can come back to life through this medium; and sicknesses are destroyed by this act.

To have hands laid on you is access to God's miracle power without any struggles. You can have what it took someone years to have just by this kingdom act. That is why you see the spirit of wisdom on Joshua because Moses laid hands on him.

"And Joshua the son of Nun was full of the spirit of wisdom; for Moses had laid his hands upon him."

It's a quicker route to receiving from God. Saul (who became Paul) received his sight after Ananias laid hands on him.

The leper was cleansed because Jesus laid hands on him.

"And there came a leper to him, beseeching him, and kneeling down to him, and saying unto him, If thou wilt, thou canst make me clean. And Jesus, moved with compassion, put forth his hand, and touched him, and saith unto him, I will; be thou clean."

Mark 1:40-41

And again

"He cometh to Bethsaida; and they bring a blind man unto him, and besought him to touch him. And he (Jesus) took the blind man by the hand, and led him out of the town; and when he had spit on his eyes, and put his hands upon him, he asked him if he saw ought. And he looked up, and said, I see men as trees, walking. After that he put his hands again upon his eyes, and made him look up: and he was restored, and saw every man clearly.   Mark 8:22-25

In Luke 13, the woman who was afflicted by the spirit of infirmity was loosed instantly and made free when Jesus laid his hands on her. (See Luke 13:11-13).

Down through the ages, not many prophets practiced this divine ordinance so Jesus before his departure renewed this principle by commanding us to do it. Go and lay hands on the sick and they shall recover.

This is a strong vehicle for divine delivery. It's express! And we see God work special miracles through the **hands** of His ministers.

THE ANOINTING OIL

"And they cast out many devils, and anointed with oil many that were sick, and healed them."

Mark 6:13

The disciples picked the oil, applied it on the body of the sick and God healed them. If God honoured that in what we call 'Bible days'; then be assured that he will honour it today as well. And there is no scripture in the Bible which forbids believers of today to apply the oil; instead, we are exhorted to keep practicing it.

"Is any sick among you?" We are exhorted, "Let him call for the elders of the church: and let them pray over him, anointing him with OIL in the name of the Lord… and the Lord will cure him."

James 5:14-15

The oil was an instrument in the time of the disciples. It is recorded in Mark 6:13 that "they… anointed with oil many that were sick, and healed them" and it was recommended to the elders to use in the name of the Lord on anybody who was sick, according to James 5:14. Do you think James wrote it because he felt high? No, the man - James was inspired by the Holy Spirit to write that, and "for our sakes, no doubt this is written". (See 1 Corinthians 9:10).

Look at it again:

"Is any sick among you? Let him call for the elders of the church; and let them pray over him, anointing him with oil in the name of the Lord"

James 5:14

53

Never doubt what has been instituted by God in His Word and don't let anybody talk you out of God's blessing. What is written is written. Is any sick among you? Let him call for the elders of the church; and let them pray over him, anointing him with Oil in the name of the Lord, and God will perform a miracle of healing in the person. The point is: **We anoint in the Name of the Lord.** We pray in His Name. So go ahead and **use** the oil. Don't **ab-use** it, but **use** it in the name of the Lord. The Christians in Corinth were taking the Holy Communion in an unworthy manner. They were **ab-using** it. Just like today many have **ab-used** the oil. Some drink it, some bath it and all sorts but that doesn't take away or nullify the ordinance of the Holy Scriptures. People need to be counselled in the practice of God's Word. Paul did it in his days and so must we in our generation.

The Word is yours to use. Put it to work and it will work for you.

"From the sole of the foot even unto the head there is no soundness in it; but wounds, and bruises, and putrifying sores: they have not been

closed, neither bound up, neither mollified with ointment." Isaiah 1:6

Have you been mollified with ointment? Pick up your oil and declare the counsel of the Lord in that house. Touch not my anointed and do my prophet no harm. The Oil is *'no harm liquid'*. If God doesn't use these natural things, then books, audio, video and other means of communicating must be discarded. But you know very well that some have received amazing insights and healing through books, listening to audio or watching a video of a man of God, among many others. I encourage you to pay attention to God, and not limit Him in anyway.

Chapter 4

IT'S A NEW DAY!

"This **is my blood, the blood of the covenant....**".
Matthew 26:28 (NET)

"T**his is my blood, which seals God's covenant....**"
Matthew 26:28 (GNT)

I particularly want to draw your attention to the fact of God's Covenant here in order to appreciate what the Holy Communion means to the Father. Jesus said the blood He shed is the blood of the covenant or the blood that seals God's covenant as the Good News Translation puts it.

When the Lord Jesus partook of the last Passover supper ever given to mankind, He closed the door of the old covenant and made way to the new covenant by giving His life on the Cross. Right after that act, the divine announcement was: **It's a new day**! The salvation of mankind has now appeared unto all which was seen by all on the cross. So let's look at some covenant truths.

COVENANT FACTS

1) *A covenant is a "binding obligation."* The Latin is *convenire,* which is "to come together or agree." The Hebrew berith is "to bind." Therefore, a covenant is the coming together or agreement between two parties. It always exists between two parties.

2) *A covenant is made with an Oath.* And an oath is an appeal to divine authority to ratify an assertion. An oath is to end all strife. The scriptures say "...an oath for the confirmation is to them an end of all strife." Hebrews 6:16. Thus where an oath is, strife shouldn't exist.

3) *A covenant carries benefits, or promises, responsibilities and obligations.* Since, there is a reason for a covenant, the parties entering into covenant must be aware of the promises and the benefits as well as the obligations.

4) *A covenant is Non-negotiable.*

"My covenant will I not break, nor alter the thing that is gone out of my lips." Psalm 89:34.

5) *A covenant ends in a Meal.*

"So come, let's make a covenant, you and I, and it will be a witness to our commitment."

Then he told his family members "Gather some stones." So they gathered stones and piled them in a heap. <u>Then Jacob and Laban sat down beside the pile of stones to eat a covenant meal.</u> (Genesis 31:44, 46 NLT).

Have you ever considered why we call it the Lord's Supper?

6) *A covenant opens a new chapter for the parties involved. That* is irrespective of the past happenings once a covenant is made, everything past is Past.

7) *A covenant offers protection*

" And you shall not only show me kindness of the Lord while I still live, that I may not die; but you shall not cut off your kindness from my house forever, no, not when the Lord has cut off every one of the enemies of David from the face of the earth."   1 Samuel 20:14-15

If a covenant between two mortals contains this level of faithfulness and kindness, what should we expect of the Most High God?

8)   *There are different types of covenants, but the blood covenant is the greatest of all.*

That is why the New Covenant, sealed by the Blood of Jesus is the most perfect, non-blemish, complete covenant ever made in human existence.

Well, I will stop here but I do hope this gives you some insight into the place of covenant in relation to the Holy Communion. That the Most High has entered into covenant with you, which cannot be dissolved by any Government, economy, danger, alarm, situation or generation. It is an eternal covenant sealed by the blood of the Lamb of God for our good. The truth is, anytime one partakes of the Holy Communion one is reminding the Most High about His irrevocable covenant, sealed by the blood of Jesus, our Passover Lamb.

And this covenant must find its fulfilment in the lives of God's people. Jesus said "I can guarantee that I won't eat it again until it finds it's fulfilment in the kingdom of God" Luke 22:16(GWT). And we are in the days of fulfilment. Friend, there is something in the Holy Communion for you that must find fulfilment in your life. So boldly lift up the cup of blessing, the blood of the covenant in solemn remembrance of the oath sworn by the Most High Himself to do you good forever.

Chapter 5

BENEFITS OF THE
HOLY COMMUNION

A benefit as defined in dictionary is an advantage, gain, profit, reward, blessing or favour. So what I mean here is the Favour, Rewards, the Profit and the Gain that come by taking the Holy Communion. The Communion is somehow a physical presence of Jesus in our lives. As we partake of it by Faith, we touch Him physically.

"For we have not an high priest which cannot be touched with the feeling of our infirmities; but was in all points tempted like as we are, yet without sin. **Let us therefore come boldly unto the throne of grace that we may obtain mercy, and find grace to help in time of need."**

Hebrews 4:15, 16 KJV

As we take it, we behold His Glory. We behold His Face shine upon us. When you come to the Table, see Him as John saw Him:

"And in the midst of the seven candlesticks one like unto the Son of man, clothed with a garment down to the foot, and girt about the paps with a golden girdle. His head and his hairs were white like wool, as white as snow; and his eyes were as a flame of fire; And his feet like unto fine brass, as if they burned in a furnace; and his voice as the sound of many waters. And he had in his right hand seven stars: and out of his mouth went a sharp two-edged sword: and his countenance was as the sun shineth in his strength.

Revelation 1:13-16

And as this **'seeing'** takes place in you, the next thing you will experience is His Mighty Healing Hands placed on you, healing every sickness and disease, destroying every infirmity and brokenness in your life. Just as He touched the blind and healed him, the same manner that He touched Peter's mother-in-law and made her whole. Just as He touched the cripple man at the pool and made him whole, so will you experience Him. See Him reach out to you. Look on Him who took all our burden and sickness away. "Looking unto Jesus the author and finisher of our faith". See Him ministering personally to you, touching you as you partake of the Holy Communion. When you see Him, You will experience His touch. This is the most Spiritual and Physical divine invitation to humiliate any force of darkness in your life.

Something will happen to you when you see Him.
Look at this from Revelation 1:17

"And when I saw him, I fell at his feet as dead. And he laid his right hand upon me, saying unto me, Fear not; I am the first and the last:"

May you encounter God. May your eyes be opened to see Him. He is sure and steadfastly faithful.

Below are some identified benefits. Remember that we only know in part, as the great Apostle stated in 1 Corinthians 13:12 **"For now we see** through a glass, darkly; but then face to face: **now I know in par**t; but then shall I know even as also I am known". No man knows the FULL benefits of the Holy Communion but the things that are revealed are for us and our children.

"The secret things belong unto the Lord our God: but those things which are revealed belong unto us and to our children for ever, that we may do all the words of this law (Deuteronomy 29:29 KJV). So we make full use of the revealed truth.

1) IT'S A FELLOWSHIP AMONG AND BETWEEN THE SAINTS WHICH BRINGS STRENGTHENING

"And Jonathan Saul's son arose, and went to David into the wood, and strengthened his hand in God."

1 Samuel 23:16

This happened because they had made a covenant sealed with a meal.

When a family keeps taking the Holy Communion together, nothing can separate them. The strength of Heaven becomes their strength. Communion fosters unity. Is there any difficulty in your family? I encourage the partaking of the Holy Communion together as a family.

Mark this: if a family cannot take communion together, they cannot walk in the strength and unity of the Lord. On the other hand, it is almost impossible for the enemy to break a family that continually take the holy communion at home. When it is taken together, you will stay together. And the situation is the same when it comes to your walk with God. It is hard to go astray if you are a communion person. The more you partake of it, the more your system is adjusted to God's Word. So take it often.

"For we being many are one bread, and one body: for we are all partakers of *that one bread*."

1 Corinthians 10:17

"And upon the first day of the week,...the disciples came together to break bread." Acts 20:7

2) THERE IS A RELEASE OF GOD'S BLESSING

The scriptures call it the "cup of blessing" in 1 Corinthians 10:16. That is every time communion is taken in faith, discerning the body, there is a release of God's Blessing. I don't care the kind of curse you might be under. It doesn't matter who has cast a spell on you, this cup is able to turn all curse into blessing. The Cup of Blessing will empower you to prevail over every adversity in life. It is God's Blessing. You cannot take the Holy Communion and not be blessed! That is why understanding is a key. You need to discern.

Just as poison will cause disturbances in a life, so The Cup of Blessing will interrupt any death in a life. That is to say this cup possesses an inherent divine substance invisible to the eyes but capable of causing reactions in you. I encourage families to take communion together to enforce and enhance unity. And because it brings unity - the blessing is released, and any element of disunity will be betrayed!

We see this in Psalm 133:

"Behold, how good and how pleasant it is for brethren to dwell together in unity! It is like the precious ointment upon the head, that ran down upon the beard, even Aaron's beard: that went down to the skirts of his garments; As the dew of Hermon, and as the dew that descended upon the mountains of Zion: for there the LORD commanded the blessing, even life for evermore."

Something happens when a family takes the Holy Communion together and be warned that the devil will do everything possible to stop you from engaging in this for he (devil) knows what will happen in that family - a strong unbreakable divine cord of unity.
See also 1Corinthians 10:16(a).

3) IT IS PART OF DIVINE WEAPON FOR SIGNS AND WONDERS

When you've done almost all you know to do, and still some diseases and sicknesses persist, go back to the Holy Communion. It is an inescapable weapon of the

Lord. The blood of Jesus is too much for any satanic host to handle. Wherever the blood was introduced, a desired breakthrough was experienced. The truth is some things delay in manifestation because of satanic resistance, and the book of Daniel makes that clear - Daniel Chapter 10. And Paul said, "…It was our will to come to you. [I mean that] I, Paul, again and again [wanted to come], but Satan hindered and impeded us. (1 Thessalonians 2:18 AMP)

The devil will always want to stop the flow of God's blessing in your life, that's why you need to mark every gate of your life with the blood by lifting the cup of blessing. When some diseases and old habits seem to gain control over your life, please lift up the bread and the cup, declaring that you are the righteousness of God in Christ Jesus - do this in faith, nothing wavering and the righteousness of God which is by faith will speak on your behalf. When His body is lifted by you in communion, healing will descend to you. It's a divine prescription for a pain free living.

"And they continued steadfastly in the apostles' doctrine and fellowship, and *breaking of bread,* and in prayers. And fear came upon every soul: and many wonders and signs were done by the apostles."

Acts 2:42-43

Did you notice that? "Many signs and wonders were done by the apostles." We have witnessed this in our ministry. We have seen hepatitis B and other blood related and skin diseases destroyed by this weapon of God. And we continue to see many signs and wonders.

4) IT IS AN AVENUE FOR AN OVERCOMING LIFE

Communion taken in faith operates in the spiritual realm, bringing to shame any satanic oppression and hindering any demonic attack. If you want to live an overcoming life, then practice this. As stated before, it is the nature and desire of satanic host to stop God's blessings in your life and to inflict pain and disorder in your life. But, continuous proclamation of your redemption through the Lord's Supper enforces your very nature to resist any satanic deployment and allow the flow of the Blessing in your life. You stake your claim through the Holy Communion.

So lift up the Blood of the Covenant and make a proclamation of the Lord in victory over every attack of darkness.

"And they overcame him (the devil) by the blood of the Lamb and by the word of their testimony..."

Revelation 12:11

Therefore, come before the communion table with the witness that "for this reason the son of God was manifested that he might destroy the work of the devil, hence every work of the devil is destroyed over my life." Name your deliverance and receive it.

5) FOR A HIGHER & BETTER LIFE

Anybody who takes the Holy Communion must be ready to walk the walk of God. You don't put a Ferrari engine into a ford fiesta, with all respect to fiesta but the two are not the same! Jesus said, just as the Father sent him and he lived by the Father even so he who eats or partake in the Holy Communion will live by Him.

"He that eateth my flesh, and drinketh my blood, dwelleth in me, and I in him. As the living Father hath sent me, and I live by the Father: so he that eateth me, even he shall live by me".

John 6:56, 57 KJV

So the taking of Holy Communion puts within you a supernatural ability, a divine blood transfusion and exchange to help overcome earthly pain and weakness. Consequently, you get ready for new life.

Paul said "...**the life which I now live in the flesh I live by the faith of the Son of God, who loved me, and gave himself for me"** (Galatians 2:20) and it was this same Paul who escaped death threatening situations several times. He was living a higher life on this earth.

6) IN COVENANT WITH THE MOST HIGH GOD

"...This cup is the new covenant between God and his people - an agreement confirmed with my blood. Do this to remember me as often as you drink it." 1 Corinthians 11:25 (NLT)

It is time to know that you are in covenant with God. The most High has entered into covenant with you, sealed by the blood of Jesus. Any time you partake of the communion, you are reminding yourself that 'hey I am in covenant with the Most High God, the creator of the heaven and earth Who has agreed to protect and deliver me, provide for me and heal me'. He is your Covenant God! So do this to waken inner-self to the Covenant. There are times we let things slip by but a return to the Lord's Supper engenders freshness of God's work in us. It pays to return for fresh encounter. In Zechariah 9, we see a great invitation and promise:

"Because of the covenant I made with you, sealed with blood, I will free your prisoners from death in a waterless dungeon. Come back to the place of safety (communion table), all you prisoners who still have hope! I promise this day that I will repay two blessings for each of your troubles." Zechariah 9:11-12(NLT)

A double blessing is promised with this covenant. Get ready for double blessing for everything you've been through. Your prisoners, even your relatives in bondage could receive deliverance under this covenant. It is time to come to the place of safety (the blood covenant - the Holy Communion) and receive restoration for every loss you incurred in the past. Weeping is over! It's time to rejoice. Just come and receive it.

7) *YOU MAKE A PROCLAMATION TO ALL THREE WORLDS OF THE LORDSHIP OF JESUS CHRIST OVER YOUR LIFE*

It is one thing to have a testimony and another to make proclamation of your testimony. When you declare or proclaim your testimony, you inflict more pain on your adversary and open doors for more victories in life. The proclamation of testimony weakens and breaks any satanic hold in other areas of your life which you might not be aware of, that's why Scripture says "they overcame by the blood of the Lamb **and** by the word of their testimony..." The word 'and' here is very important in understanding the concept and the secret to their victory over the adversary. It was the blood **plus** the word of their testimony. There is a conflation factor!

The Blood and their testimony! The Blood is there, but if you don't make a proclamation of your freedom through the Blood, things might be difficult. Don't separate THESE TWO THINGS: The Blood and the Word of their Testimony. Victory comes through that.

A testimony is to witness a solemn statement made under oath. It also means evidence, admission, or a show. The Holy Communion is your evidence or 'a show' of God's deliverance in your life, not your feelings. So lift the Cup and make a proclamation. Be a witness by partaking of the Holy Communion. And that declaration you make permeates into the three worlds where certain rulers exist.

Look at it:

"This is why God has given him an exceptional honor - the name honored above all other names - so that at the name of Jesus **everyone in heaven, on earth, and in the world below** will kneel and confess that Jesus Christ is Lord to the glory of God the Father".

Philippians 2:9-11(GWT)

Your declaration of the Lordship of Jesus Christ through the Holy Communion over your life to the world around you is a key to an overcoming life. At the Communion, you make a proclamation to the world around you about the Lordship of Jesus Christ over your life. Your claim is "He rules over my life." Your affirmation is "principalities and powers are disarmed over my life".

You cause an uplift of the lordship of Jesus over your life by partaking of the Holy Communion.

"And there are three that bear witness in earth, the spirit, and the water, and the blood: and these three agree in one." 1 John 5:8

The blood is your witness, so testify of it by taking the Holy Communion. And it will speak for you anytime, any-day, anywhere. It is the evidence of your victory. This scripture above is one of our bases for belief of the efficacy of the blood. The blood - one with the spirit will lift up a standard against the enemy.

"...When the enemy shall come in like a flood, The Spirit of the Lord shall lift up a standard against him." Isaiah 59:19

"For every time you eat this bread and drink this cup, you are representing and signifying and *proclaiming* the fact of the Lord's death until He comes again."

1 Corinthians 11:26(AMP)

8) FOR STRENGTH

When I speak of strength, don't just be limited to physical strength. My focus here is a condition of potency in every area of your life, the state where you are able to resist any force contrary to the will of God. "For he that eateth and drinketh unworthily, eateth and drinketh damnation to himself, not discerning the Lord's body. For this cause many are **weak** and sickly among you, and many sleep." 1 Corinthians 11:29-30

God meant that we partake of the Lord's body for strength and not weakness. And, there is a cause for the weakness (weakness of any area) among us, which is not the will of God. The strain of weakness and sickness is meant to be silenced by the body of the Lord. But because of lack of discerning the Lord's body, many have legitimized weakness in their lives. The truth is after you've received your healing from the Lord you will need to be strong to continue to resist the adversary. The enemy's desire is to cause God's people to lose what they receive from God, but strength in God will help you refuse to comply with any satanic tricks. And you effectuate that by taking the communion in a worthy manner. That's discerning the Lord's Body. God wants us to walk in Divine Health and not just getting healed.

Elijah was fed by the angel of the Lord and he went forty days without food. He went in the strength of that divine food. Take communion and move on.

9) FOR DIVINE HEALTH

"For he that eateth and drinketh unworthily, eateth and drinketh damnation to himself, not discerning the Lord's body. <u>For this cause</u> many are weak and <u>sickly</u> among you, and many asleep."

1 Corinthians 11:29-30

If many were sick because they did not discern the Lord's body, then by discerning the body you guarantee yourself divine health.

Your Healing has been provided in the communion. His body was broken that yours shouldn't be broken.

The wine (blood) unblocks any blocks in the arteries so your heart will function properly so as to ensure you are delivered from any cardiac arrest. You execute a divine blood transfusion at the communion table to ensure divine health, for they are health to all their flesh. (See Proverbs 4:20-22).

Look at this:

"I am the living bread which came down from heaven: if any man eats of this bread, he shall live for ever: and the bread that I will give is my flesh, which I will give for the life of the world. The Jews therefore strive among themselves, saying, how can this man give us his flesh to eat? Then Jesus said unto them, Verily, verily, I say unto you, Except ye

eat the flesh of the Son of man, and drink his blood, ye have no life in you. Whoso eateth my flesh, and drinketh my blood, hath eternal life; and I will raise him up at the last day. For my flesh is meat indeed, and my blood is drink indeed. He that eateth my flesh, and drinketh my blood, dwelleth in me, and I in him. As the living Father hath sent me, and I live by the Father: so he that eateth me, even he shall live by me. This is that bread which came down from heaven: not as your fathers did eat manna, and are dead: he that eateth of this bread shall live for ever."   John 6:51-59

Receiving your healing and walking in divine health is God's Will for our lives, and the Holy Communion is our direct access to this. We make undistorted contact with the fullness of His Personality.

"But he was pierced for our rebellion, crushed for our sins. He was beaten so we could be whole. He was whipped so we could be healed."

Isaiah 53:5 NLT

The Lord Jesus suffered for our wholeness. He was whipped so we could be healed. The marrow of the Holy Communion could be summarised in this: *He was pierced for our rebellion, crushed for our sins. He was beaten so we could be whole. He was whipped so we could be healed.*

10) THERE IS LONG LIFE IN THE HOLY COMMUNION

Looking again at 1 Corinthians 11:29-30, we find another startling truth:

"For he that eateth and drinketh unworthily, eateth and drinketh damnation to himself, not discerning the Lord's body. <u>For this cause</u> many are weak and sickly among you, and many <u>asleep</u> (dead)". That is many were even dead for this cause. Or put it this way: untimely death could have been abrogated if people discerned the Lord's body.

And in John 6:56-58 Jesus said:

"He that eateth my flesh, and drinketh my blood, dwelleth in me, and I in him. As the living Father hath sent me, and I live by the Father: so he that

eateth me, even he shall live by me. This is that bread which came down from heaven: not as your fathers did eat manna, and are dead: he that eateth of this bread shall live for ever."

And "with long life will I satisfy him, and show him my salvation." Psalm 91:16

The truth is you can neutralise the threat of untimely death. The Holy Communion is quid pro quo, you take it and you'll receive life. Taking communion is a legal spiritual act which has great spiritual and physical significance; and all the beings in heaven, earth and earth beneath know that. If food poison can harm you, then communion will send great health rewards into your system. When you get satisfied at the 'table', you will be satisfied in life. At the Communion Table any toxic substance in your system which is responsible for unnecessary ageing and untimely death is extinct. Remember, it was eating that brought about death in human race and it will take another 'eating' to cancel that threat and introduce life. Jesus said "...he that eats of this bread shall live forever." What the disobedience of the first Adam brought, is undone by the obedience of the last Adam.

Look at this:

"And Elisha came again to Gilgal: and there was a dearth in the land; and the sons of the prophets were sitting before him: and he said unto his servant, Set on the great pot, and seethe pottage for the sons of the prophets. And one went out into the field to gather herbs, and found a wild vine, and gathered thereof wild gourds his lap full, and came and shred them into the pot of pottage: for they knew them not. So they poured out for the men to eat. And it came to pass, as they were eating of the pottage, that they cried out, and said, O thou man of God, there is death in the pot. And they could not eat thereof. But he said, Then bring meal. And he (Elisha) cast it into the pot; and he said, Pour out for the people, that they may eat. And there was no harm in the pot."

(See 2 Kings 4:38-41)

"And there was no harm in the pot."

Here, the 'Meal' was the instrument of healing used in curing any harm found in the pot. It was a vehicle - carrying God's healing power to deal with the threat of the devil in that pot.

In Proverbs 9:1-5; Wisdom says there is a meal prepared for us to partake of and walk in an uncommon wisdom. "Come eat of my bread, and drink of the wine which I have mingled." verse 5. So there is a prepared meal! There is a table set for you to silence your enemies. There, you shall be satisfied with long life.

11) YOU ANOINT YOUR FAITH WHEN YOU TAKE COMMUNION

There is a degree of invigoration, robustness and anointing that comes with taking the Communion.

"My heart panted, fearfulness affrighted me: the night of my pleasure hath he turned into fear unto me. *Prepare the table,* watch in the watchtower, *eat, drink: arise, ye princes, and anoint the shield."*   Isaiah 21:4-5

86

And Ephesians 6:16 says "In every situation take the <u>shield of faith</u>, and with it you will be able to extinguish all the flaming arrows of the devil."

Here in Isaiah 21:5 is a prophetic instruction for the believers of today about how to strengthen our faith (shield of faith), yet many despise it. The word *table* in verse 5 according to Strong's Concordance is *shulchan* which means a meal, therefore the preparation of the table (meal - the communion) is paramount to our walk of faith.

When fear seem to be on the rise against you or whenever you are caught in the claws of worry - legitimately prepare the table and get your faith anointed to flush out threat of fear. You mark it! Haven't you ever experienced a sense of calmness within you anytime you partake of the Holy Communion? There is an anointing that flows down to you from Him when you make the most unparalleled contact with His body through the Holy Communion which destroys fear. Now after the eating and drinking, the next thing is to declare what you see, for your faith is at another level.

God said in verse 6 of Isaiah 21 that after the table (meal) has been prepared and eating and drinking is done **"let him declare what he sees."** After the meal, something happens to your inner man which sets you up for divine utterances. Divine boldness takes hold of you for divine articulations, and you are the one to make declarations of what you see through the Holy Communion. You don't just take communion and keep quiet; your mouth must utter some things, for it is written "thou shall also decree a thing, and it shall be established unto thee; and when men are cast down, then **shall thou say**, there is a lifting up." Job 22:28-29.

Don't let fear overcome you. You are delivered from it therefore, get the table ready, eat the bread and drink the cup, and you will see how your shield of faith would be anointed against the weapon of fear. Is there any threat of the enemy in any area of your life? Prepare the table of the Lord, take the communion and the power of God's Spirit will surge into your being afresh for freedom. *When Faith springs up, fear will break off.*

12) FOR IMPARTATION OF DIVINE WISDOM

Communion is a divine invitation to partake of the wisdom of God available for you. My practice is to pray in tongues and take the Holy Communion any time I have a major decision to make, because almost all problems are wisdom problems. If we knew the 'how' to life issues; mistakes, regrets and pain will be hindered in our lives. The bible says "The labour of the foolish wearieth every one of them, because he knoweth not how…" Therefore, it is important to have the 'know how', and wisdom will deliver that into your hands. Do you know that wisdom is profitable to direct? Ecclesiastes 10:10.

"Riches and honour are with me, enduring wealth and righteousness" says wisdom. "My fruit is better than gold, yes, than refined gold, and my increase than choice silver." She continues: "those that find me find life and I will cause them to inherit riches and fill their treasuries." (See Proverbs 8). So, wisdom becomes a must in the race of life. And when you come to the table of the Lord, you receive this impartation of wisdom.

May I repeat this? One of the ways to receive wisdom is to partake of the Holy Communion. It is one of God's provided avenues for his children to walk in wisdom.

Look at this:

"Wisdom hath builded her house, She hath hewn out her seven pillars: She hath killed her beasts; she hath mingled her wine; She hath also furnished her table. She hath sent forth her maidens: She crieth upon the highest places of the city, Whoso is simple, let him turn in hither: As for him that wanteth understanding, she saith to him, _**Come, eat of my bread, And drink of the wine which I have mingled.**_ **Forsake the foolish, and live; And go in the way of understanding.**

Proverbs 9:1-6

There is the invitation – "come; eat of my bread and drink of the wine" and wisdom shall be yours. With regards to taking communion, there are many who are

90

not walking in this understanding but don't let them sway you. "Forsake the foolish, and live" the scripture says in verse 6 and "go in the way of understanding." Receive the impartation of Wisdom and it will justify you in the end.

13) YOU TRIGGER ANGELIC MINISTRATION

Looking at Exodus 12, it seems to me that there is a close relationship between the Blood and ministry of Angels, as the Angel of the Lord was dispatched to Passover those who were blood-marked.

And since angels only obey the voice of the Word of God, your world will be saturated by their presence if you will continually come before the Table of the Lord. Do you remember the chariot of fire and horses of fire in 2 Kings 2:11? Well, this divine presence has not gone away because of the new covenant. Angels still minister for the heirs of salvation.

Hebrews 1:13-14 states there is a charge unto angels to minister for us.

"But to which of the angels said he at any time, Sit on my right hand, until I make thine enemies thy footstool? Are they not all ministering spirits, sent forth to minister for them who shall be heirs of salvation?"

Hebrews 1:13-14

And when you obey God by taking the communion in faith (because Jesus said - this do: referring to the Holy Communion) you trigger Angelic ministration. The simple reason for this is because Angels are designed to obey the voice of God's Word. **"Bless the Lord, ye his angels,... hearkening unto the voice of his word."** (That's Psalm 103:20). Thus your obedience to God's Word provokes angelic ministration in your life. Once you obey the Word, Angels will work in your Life. It's a divine law! When you put the Word to work, Angels will go to work on your behalf executing all the plan of God for your life. And beware - nothing can stop them! They excel in strength.

"Bless the Lord, ye his angels that excel in strength, that do his commandments, hearkening unto the voice of his word."

Psalm 103:20 KJV

14) COMMUNION - BETTER THAN MANNA

Hear what Jesus said:

"I am the living bread which came down from heaven: if any man eat of this bread, he shall live forever: and the bread that I will give is my flesh, which I will give for the life of the world. The Jews therefore strive among themselves, saying, how can this man give us his flesh to eat? Then Jesus said unto them, Verily, verily, I say unto you, except you eat the flesh of the Son of man, and drink his blood, you have no life in you. Whoso eats my flesh, and drinks my blood, has eternal life; and I will raise him up at the last day. For my flesh is meat indeed, and my blood is drink indeed. He who eats my flesh, and drinks my blood, dwells in me, and I in him. As the living Father sent me, and I live because of the Father, so he who feeds on me, will live because of me. This is that bread which came down from heaven: not as your fathers did eat manna, and are dead: he who eats this bread shall live forever."

John 6:51-59

It must be noted that the people of God ate manna in the wilderness and the scriptures clearly state that there was none feeble among them. (Psalm 105:37). Manna was their daily diet and it completely destroyed weakness and feebleness among them. Psalm 78:25 says everyone ate the bread of the mighty - man ate angels' food (AMP). Taking manna was their prescription to stay cured, healthy and whole. However, the people had to gather according to the instruction of God. If the old covenant could provide that power to heal and make people strong, then it can be said that taking the body of the Lord in the new covenant will have better result, because, it is of a better covenant. We are not eating bread of angels but the Living Bread which is plenary, full of grace and truth. We have purging of the mind and Healing of the body in the Communion.

15) YOU MAKE A SHOW

"For as often as ye eat this bread, and drink this cup, ye do *show* the Lord's death till he come."

1 Corinthians 11:26

The word "show", again from Vine's Complete Expository Dictionary of Old and New Testament Words means: to exhibit, to show by making known. It also means to show by way of proving.

And it also means to declare, preach or speak of according to Strong's Concordance. That means, when you partake of the communion, you make prove of your healing. It is the certificate of your healing from all oppression of the devil.

As you eat the bread and drink the cup, you are showing *something* in the realm of the spirit that the Lord Jesus died and rose for your justification; therefore every hold of Satan over your life is broken. The curse is broken over your life. This is how you invoke the efficacy of his death in your life, and it is the certificate or proof of your redemption so lift the cup as a proof of God's forgiveness and wholeness in your life.

You have to see that the blood of Jesus perpetuates the work of Jesus in your life. It is as though Jesus Christ is 'physically' present with you, hence hear Him proclaim "You are Healed". For the life of the flesh is in the blood.

16) *FOR REVELATION & ILLUMINATION*

Jesus becomes more real to you and you will recognize Him more when you obey his commission to 'do' in remembrance of him. Take the bread and you'll understand the scriptures.

Taking communion is receiving the doctrine of the Kingdom of God. Abraham was offered bread and wine by Melchizedek (that is Genesis 14:18-20), and right after that act we see Abraham did something he had never done before because up till that moment the light had not come to him. He tithed after receiving the bread and the wine (symbolic of communion) from Melchizedek who was the type of Christ the King - Priest. Hebrews 6:20 says "whither the forerunner is for us entered, even Jesus, made an high priest for ever after the order of Melchizedek." When Abraham was given the bread by the high priest of God (Melchizedek) a kingdom doctrine (an illumination) was imparted into him, kingdom light penetrated his being and that's why you find him doing something he had never done before all his life. Oh! That we will come to the Lord's Supper discerning His body, how different things will be.

Luke 24:15 states: "And it came to pass, that, while they communed together and reasoned, Jesus himself drew near, and went with them."

Now look at this:

"Then he said unto them, O fools, and slow of heart to believe all that the prophets have spoken: Ought not Christ to have suffered these things, and to enter into his glory? <u>And beginning at Moses and all the prophets, he expounded unto them in all the scriptures the things</u>

concerning himself. And they drew nigh unto the village, whither they went: and he made as though he would have gone further. But they constrained him, saying, Abide with us: for it is toward evening, and the day is far spent. **And he went in to tarry with them. And it came to pass, as he sat at meat with them, he took bread, and blessed it, and brake, and gave to them. And their eyes were opened, and they knew him; and he vanished out of their sight.**

Luke 24:25-31 KJV

Please note that though Jesus expounded the scriptures to them as stated in verse 27, they still couldn't recognise him (as the Lord Jesus) until after the bread was broken. There is some illuminating effect about the bread that darkness can't handle. The communion has a quickening ability that every believer ought to benefit from. The time of walking in darkness is over. When light (truth) is missing, mourning is the result. Job said "I went mourning without the sun (light)..." Job 30:28. Friend, the result of darkness is grievous, atrocious and cataclysmic. It is when light is missing that mourning sets in. But your light has come!

And the root cause of certain core issues in your life will be revealed to you so you can deal with them.

The scriptures shall be opened to you so you can walk in the light of the Word, and that's when winning begins. Operating in revelation and insight makes you unbeatable and you will never be defeated another day in your life, because you now employ certain strategies unknown to your adversaries architected by the encounter at the table.

When revelation hits your camp, the glory of the Lord will invade your world and suddenly you begin to see things in a new way. That glory (illuminating power) of God will dispel every gloom out of any world. The truth is, every true ruler has Light and it is by His light that you will truly rule in life.

The man considered to be the greatest of all men of the east in his time said "**by his light I walked through**

darkness;" (Job 29:3 KJV). When light emerges, darkness is dispelled. This is your hour!

17) IT HAS ETERNAL VALUE

It is categorically stated that Jesus shall drink with you and me again. You see, we are given something that is very dear to the Lord.

"But I say unto you, I will not drink henceforth of this fruit of the vine, until that day when I drink it new <u>with you</u> in my Father's kingdom.   Matthew 26:29

Believers shall continue to partake of the Holy Communion even years to come. We all shall join the master to drink again "the fruit of the vine". Oh what a blessing! How I wish we knew the depth of this in the Father's heart?

Years after we are gone, we will still be taking part in this Kingdom practice, this everlasting covenant. All of us shall join the Master to celebrate the triumph of His blood. Hallelujah!

"Now the God of peace, that brought again from the dead our Lord Jesus, that great shepherd of the sheep, through the blood of the everlasting covenant, make you perfect in every good work to do His will, working in you that which is well pleasing in His sight, through Jesus Christ; to whom be glory forever and ever. Amen.

Hebrews 13:20-21

18) AFTER THE ORDER OF MELCHIZEDEK

"And Melchizedek king of Salem brought forth bread and wine: and he was the priest of the most high God. And he blessed him, and said, Blessed be Abram of the most high God, possessor of heaven and earth: And blessed be the most high God, which hath delivered thine enemies into thy hand. And he gave him tithes of all".

Genesis 14:18-20

"And no man taketh this honour unto himself, but he that is called of God, as was Aaron. So also Christ glorified not himself to be made an high priest; but he that said unto him, Thou art my Son, today have I begotten thee. As he saith also in another place, Thou art a priest for ever after the order of Melchizedek."

Hebrews 5:4-6

Bread is symbolic of doctrine, and Jesus speaking of the doctrine of the Pharisees said "beware of the leaven of the Pharisees" referring to their doctrine. Therefore when Melchizedek gave Abraham bread, he gave Abraham the doctrine of the Kingdom. Melchizedek taught Abraham something pertaining to God's Kingdom and after receiving that doctrine, as pointed out before, you find Abraham doing something he had never done before and that was to tithe which opens the floodgates of heaven. When you bring yourself faithfully before the Table of the Lord, certain instructions and leading will come to you which will bring about breakthroughs and victories you never thought were possible. In your walk of faith, divine direction is very important.

"...And he (Abraham) gave him tithes of all."
(Genesis 14:20)

The Lord's Supper does something to your spiritual being. It imparts kingdom principles into you. There are things you will only have the urge and the strength to do exclusively after you've taken the Holy Communion. There are some things that no man can teach you or corroborate. You only get them by revelation. Apostle Paul said in the letter to the Galatians chapter 2 verses 2 that he went up by revelation. Make no mistake about it - there are some breakthroughs and lifting that will solely take place by revelation. You will go up by revelation, for what comes from above is above all. Not until after Abraham had received the bread and the wine, he had no idea about tithing which carries a unique generational blessing.

Friend, the honour of partaking in the bread and the wine from the Master as did Abraham in Genesis 14 shown above is given to us by the Father. And when we do this - we activate the blessing of Abraham. We become possessor of every benefit, our enemies are delivered into our hands, and we receive the impartation to walk in Kingdom principles.

Already gone <u>in there</u> for us, our Lord Jesus is the chief priest forever in the order of Melchizedek. (Hebrews 6:20 GWT). He is the King of Salem (Peace), so we can have peace. That is why we find such a powerful decree: "Now the Lord of peace Himself give you peace always by all means." 2 Thessalonians 3:16. Look at that: Peace always by all means! Whatever it takes for you to have peace the Lord will do, because you are in covenant with Him. Your all round peace is his priority, and he will give you peace by all means.

19) REMEMBER HIM - OUR SAVIOUR

"And when he had given thanks, he broke it, and said, Take, eat: this is my body, which is broken for you: this do in remembrance of me. After the same

manner also he took the cup, when he had supped, saying, This cup is the new testament in my blood: this do ye, as oft as ye drink it, in remembrance of me."

1 Corinthians 11:24 -25

He said, "this do in remembrance of me." In taking the bread and the cup, we remember the Lord. The question is: who is Jesus and why and what should we remember? One may say He is the Son of God - True. Well, that is not all that He wants us to remember of Him. Others may say he died on the cross; good but that's not all. If we take a step back into the Old Testament, we are called upon to "Remember our creator..." (Ecclesiastes 12:1). Now if we look again in John 1:3 we find that all things were made by Jesus. Thus, Jesus Christ is the Creator of all things; and he wants us to remember His creative ability to recreate new things in us anytime we partake of the Holy Communion. He is able to fill any void and emptiness in our lives. He is able to recreate any organ in our body which is on the wane. When Jesus said "Do this in remembrance of me", he meant we should call to mind who HE IS. HE IS THE GREAT I AM. The creator - who can create new hearts, kidneys, lungs, productive organs, eyes and so on. He can create a heart in you that will love even the most unlovable people beyond your wildest imagination. When the blind Bartimaeus needed new eyes, Jesus gave him new ones. When the man at the pool had lost his ability to walk, The Creator (Jesus Christ) our Lord created new strength and ability in those legs to walk again. And He said "His body is given for you (us)" hence our eyes must be set on Him - reminding us of the freedom and wealth he brought to us from above. Our minds must be full of the wealth of peace he brought. For our sake he became poor that we might be made rich. This He wants us to remember not our sins. He broke the curse of the law so we can live in the blessing - this is what Jesus wants us to be mindful of and not our weakness. He was pierced for our rebellion, crushed for our sins; beaten so we could be whole, whipped so we could be healed. He was made sin for us, who knew no sin; that we might become the righteousness of God in Him. This again, is what He wants us to remember and be conscious of and not to be sin conscious.

Never, ever forget that you are the righteousness of God and He has qualified you for all of God's blessings. Therefore, as you partake of the Holy Communion, release your faith for His creative ability to be operative in you.

"So now there is no condemnation for those who belong to Christ Jesus. And because you belong to him, the power of the life-giving Spirit has freed you from the power of sin that leads to death."

(Romans 8:1, 2 NLT)

The threat of death is swallowed up by His life. Therefore REMEMBER HIM.

20) DEAL WITH EVERY GUILT (Get Washed)

The power of the blood that cleansed even the heavenly things will wash you any day. It will make you presentable before the throne in spite of your fallings and short comings. Look at this:

"I answered him, "Sir, you know." Then he told me, "These are the people who are coming out of the terrible suffering. They have washed their robes and made them white in the blood of the lamb. <u>That is why they are in front of the throne of God</u>. They serve him day and night in his temple. The one who sits on the throne will spread his tent over them. They will never be hungry or thirsty again. Neither the sun nor any burning heat will ever overcome them. The lamb in the centre near the throne will be their shepherd. He will lead them to springs filled with the water of life, and God will wipe every tear from their eyes."

Revelation 7:14-17 GWT

That's why they are in front of the Throne of God. There is a reason why they are in front of the Throne and *the Blood of the Lamb is that reason.* Listen Friend, the Blood of Jesus puts you in front, protects and brings fulfilment into your life. If you are going to be in front of health and wholeness, you must understand the place of the Holy Communion in your life. You are **Forgiven**, **Washed**, **Cleaned** and **Sanctified** and set apart for mercy. You will be surprised how many Christians are plagued with the feeling of guilt but guilt has no place at the communion table, so don't allow it in you! Here in lies the victory of the saints.

Through the blood of Jesus, we have our Redemption. Through the blood we have Forgiveness. Through the blood we are Cleansed. Through the blood we are Justified. Through the blood we are Sanctified. (Ephesians 1:7; John 1:7; Romans 5:9 & Hebrews 13:12). This is the Victory! So we can boldly say there is therefore now no condemnation against us. The Lamb of God has taken care of us. Oh what a Joy unspeakable! The Blood puts me in front of the throne, and the Most High spreads His tent over me. Hallelujah.

Chapter 6

THE BLOODLINE-THE LIFELINE

In following the instruction of the Lord, it became needful to bring to your attention the power of drawing the Bloodline. This is pleading the blood of Jesus over every area of your life and all that pertains to you. It is setting a divine demarcation and boundary that no foe can cross over. It's a kind of believers' act that *insure* all that belongs to the believer by enforcing the Blood bought victory of the Lord Jesus Christ over all forces of darkness; ensuring every evil intentions, plans, calculations and all diabolical meetings and intelligence are overruled. Thus, you establish your legal right of peace and wholeness through the blood in the Name of Jesus.

It must therefore be stated that, God has always been drawing this line in human existence. He did that in the Garden of Eden when man sinned. A Bloodline was drawn when Cain killed Abel, and that line wouldn't let Cain escape. There was Bloodline drawn when God entered into Covenant with Abraham, and we see it drawn again when God was bringing the children of Israel from Egypt. As the scriptures tell us, all forms of miracles were done but Pharaoh wouldn't let go of the people. But as soon as the Bloodline was drawn, a release came. The enemy couldn't hold any longer when the blood was introduced. I see a release of your wealth into your hands in Jesus' Name. I see every demonic hold over your life broken now, something is happening to you now as you are reading this book!

In Zechariah 9:11-12, God made reference to the Bloodline and said as for thee also, because of the blood of the covenant your prisoners shall go free. The book of Hebrews teaches of the Bloodline drawn all the way up to the heavens to purge the heavenly things and no contamination could cross over the Blood. As you partake of the Holy Communion, know that no contamination can cross over the Blood to you. The Blood is your Seal.

This is it: "then he said, this blood confirms the covenant God has made with you. And in the same way, he sprinkled blood on the Tabernacle and on everything used for worship. In fact, according to the Law of Moses, nearly everything was purified with blood. For without the shedding of blood, there is no forgiveness. That is why the Tabernacle and everything in it, which were copies of things in heaven, had to be purified by the blood of animals. But the real things in heaven had to be purified with far better sacrifices than the blood of animals". (Hebrews 9:20-23 NLT).

And Luke 22:20 states: "…This cup is the new covenant in my blood, which is shed for you." Jesus said "…my blood…is for you."

If His blood is for me, then I can use it. That's why you find in the book of Revelation that they used the blood to overcome the enemy. They overcame by the blood of the Lamb and by the word of their testimony, so plead the blood!

When one lifts up the cup of blessing, you instantly call for heaven's attention. All heaven respond to the Blood.

An account in Exodus 12:1-23 clearly teaches us that evil passed over wherever the Bloodline was drawn. When the people of Israel obeyed the voice of God and applied the blood on their doorposts, no evil dared. They were kept safe and secured in their houses and territories. In fact, it's in the blood that we have our protection.

Whenever the blood is applied, a great gulf is instantly fixed between you (the applicant) and your adversary, though they (your adversaries) can see you but cannot access you. (Luke 16:26). A strong hedge of protection is built over and around the person or anything you plead the blood upon. (Do you remember the account in Job 1:10?). You cannot be toyed with as long as the blood is upon you and the devil knows it. The blood guaranteed the security of the Israelites on the night of danger and the mass destruction in Egypt. And if we have a better covenant, we should expect more from the

Blood that was shed before the foundation of the world; the blood that speaks better things than the blood of Abel.

By faith, in the name of Jesus, draw a blood line over and around anything that relates to you and this blood can stop or abate any judgement. The Life of God is in it, the Word of God is on it. Therefore, demand the reconciliation of all things in your life knowing that "all things are reconciled through the blood" (See Colossians 1:20). Plead the winning blood, and mark the doorpost of your life. Your spirit, soul and body must come under the protective power of the blood in these last days.

Our responsibility is to "sprinkle the blood" and the power that resides in the blood of Jesus will go to work on our behalf. One woman of God wrote "As soon as we are awakened in the morning we should cry (plead) for the Blood to be upon us, within us, around us; and between us and all evil and the author of evil." And she continued, "The last thing before we sleep should be in the same way - the protection of the Blood." I believe this will stop the devil from throwing dreams and visions and junk of darkness that we have no business with. Live in the Blood Covenant sealed in heaven. Any time you are faced with any satanic oppression and danger, lift the proof of your redemption and declare your eternal triumph purchased by the blood of the everlasting covenant and never back off until you see the victory. Time is nothing compared to the victory that will come to you. How long or short you stand, should not be your focus but The Word of God, which *cannot* fail.

When we plead the blood, the wicked one is rendered powerless and ineffective.

Apply the Blood, and death will bow, sickness will flee, afflictions will melt away, and ashes will turn to beauty, brass to gold and iron to silver. Total peace shall be over your walls, violence shall no more be heard in your territory. There shall be no wasting or destruction within the borders but everlasting praise shall be your gates. When the Bloodline is drawn - you live in the realm of

God where "the evil one touches you not." This is how you overrule forces of darkness and render every enemy helpless. (Revelation 12:11).

It is your Passover to cross-over any form of danger.

Pray this prayer. In the Name of Jesus, I plead the blood of Jesus over my life, family, home, house and all possessions; against any influence of Satan, and I nullify, dismantle and oppose any diabolic movements, operations, manoeuvres, manipulations and plans against me and all that relate to me. By the blood of Jesus, I overrule any divination, spells and enchantments against my life and family. By faith, I release the power of the blood of Jesus to work and speak in my favour and against all that rise against me. In the Name of Jesus.

How Often Do I Need to take the Communion and the Manner?

Let's look at the *HOW* or the manner first. Everything in the Kingdom of God is done by faith. When it is done in faith, it pleases the Father. Faith is what gets His attention, so communion must be taken in faith.

To expatiate this, there is one law that is required anytime you come to the Table, and that is the Law of Faith. This is because, "...he that cometh to God must believe." God requires you to believe when you come to His Table. So the law of Faith must be put to work. How? By taking it worthily; and that is done by treating the bread and the cup as **uncommon** things which carry your healing, wholeness and forgiveness. This is how to put the law of faith to work at the Table.

It all works by the law of faith. "Through faith he kept the Passover and the sprinkling of blood..." (Hebrews 11:28) "By what law? of works? Nay: but by the law of faith." Romans 3:27 and Romans 4:16 say "Therefore it is of faith, that it might be by grace; to the end the promise might be sure to all the seed..." Consequently, Hebrews 11:6 states:

"But without faith it is impossible to please him: for he that cometh to God must believe that He is, and that He is a Rewarder of them that diligently seek Him." Therefore do not half-heartedly take communion as most Christians do. Show faith in the Son of God by receiving every benefit of his death on the cross. This attitude of faith is what you need in partaking of the Holy Communion.   The word *unworthily* as indicated in 1 Corinthians 11:27   according to Vine's Complete Expository Dictionary of Old and New Testament Words means treating it as a common meal, the bread and the cup as common things, not apprehending their solemn symbolic import. The bread and the cup are not common things. So your attitude matters. The attitude of faith, the readiness and willingness to discern what this meal means to your earthly walk. For the measure and degree of honour and respect you show at the Table will determine the flow of God's Virtue and Grace to you. And that's exactly what Jesus meant when He said in Mark 4:24 "**...with the same measure you use, it will be measured to you;**"

To treat the Lord's body as nothing is to despise your very own wholeness in life.

There is importation of freshness of divine life into your life, whenever you take communion. So do not turn off God's provision for total health and perfect soundness by treating it like a common meal. It's a covenant meal, a divine meal given to bring wholeness to your life. Therefore, discern the body of the Lord; that by His stripes you are healed. That He was bruised for our iniquity and the chastisement of our peace was upon Him. This is what it means to worthily partake of the Lord's Supper.

HOW OFTEN?

"And let us not be weary in well doing…" Galatians 6:9
"For I have received of the Lord that which also I delivered unto you, That the Lord Jesus the same night in which he was betrayed took bread: And when he had

given thanks, he brake it, and said, Take, eat: this is my body, which is broken for you: this do in remembrance of me. After the same manner also he took the cup, when he had supped, saying, This cup is the new testament in my blood: this do ye, as oft as ye drink it, in remembrance of me. *For as often as ye eat this bread, and drink this cup,* you do show the Lord's death till he comes."

1 Corinthians 11:23-26

The question is: how *often* would you like to do something that is good for you? How *often* would you practice something that you know is best for you? Well the answer is solely with you. It exclusively depends on you.

How often you take communion depends entirely on you. But the word *often* means: *many times at short intervals.* That doesn't sound like once a month to me. Moreover, some of the definitions given for *often* are: *repeatedly* or *every day.* And Acts 2:46 affirms they practised this daily. "And day after day they regularly assembled in the temple with united purpose, and in their homes they broke bread [including the Lord's Supper]. (AMP). However, it must be stated that there is no biblical formula stating how many times a day or how many times a week or how many times a month we should partake of it. So, I will leave the rest for your personal conviction. How often **largely** depends on you. You decide, but you make sure you take it as often as possible.

Smith Wigglesworth, the Apostle of Faith who had at least 19 recorded raising of the dead in his ministry was known to have taken communion daily. And that showed in his life and ministry of faith. And as pointed out under benefits of communion earlier, you anoint your faith when you take the Holy Communion. Smith Wigglesworth had such a great faith that achieved towering results for the Kingdom of God. So you decide, and when you do be not weary in well doing, for in due season you shall reap, knowing that the Holy Communion is a Commission. It is as important as the Preaching of the Gospel. It is part of our Kingdom practice. The Master said *"this do in remembrance of me"* and that is a command that we must obey with love and passion.

So you don't have to wait till your church is taking communion before. Take it at home. Gather the family for communion, as a priest of the Lord. This communion (practice) can be taken/done anywhere convenient for you and never stop doing that till He comes. Do it often and receive the full benefit of it.

"*For as often as you eat this bread, and drink this cup, you do show the Lord's death till he comes.*"

"Now the God of peace, that brought again from the dead our Lord Jesus, that great shepherd of the sheep, **through the blood of the everlasting covenant,** Make you perfect in every good work to do his will, working in you that which is well pleasing in his sight, through Jesus Christ; to whom be glory forever and ever. Amen." (Hebrews 13:20, 21)

The Prayer:

Prepare the Bread and the Cup and make pronouncement of the blessings of God.

Father, I come to you today, in the Name of Jesus, I thank you and I believe in my heart and confess with my mouth that my Lord Jesus Christ died and rose for complete redemption of my life. I confess this day that I'm delivered from.......... (*put any area you want God's manifestation, e.g. deliverance from sickness, diseases, poverty etc.*)**. I receive Healing in my body, Wealth for my life, increase, favour, and sound mind. Financial abundance, deliverance and wholeness and I partake in full, all that Jesus died on the cross for. The fruit of the Spirit and the Gifts of the Spirit all manifest in my Life. I acknowledge this day the power of the Blood Covenant in my life. This is for my health and forgiveness; for my lifting and promotion. It is for the harvest of uncommon wisdom and strength in my life, for as my days so shall my strength be. I receive divine direction for**

my life. By faith, I give thanks and praise you, in Jesus Name.

Now, by Faith take the bread and say Heavenly Father "The Lord Jesus the same night He was betrayed took bread: gave thanks and broke it, and said, Take, eat: This is My Body, broken for you: this do in remembrance of me" Therefore, Father I give you thanks and confess this day that I partake of His Body and receive the Fullness of God's Blessing (Then eat the Bread. Remember you are taking the bread from Him. For He said, Take, eat This is My Body. Matthew 26:26. So see Him reach out to you);

Likewise, By Faith Lift the Cup, Thank Him and pray: In the Name of Jesus I receive Forgiveness based on the authority of your Word in areas I've missed the mark. As I drink this cup, I observe my total Healing, Forgiveness and Fullness of Your Blessing in this Blood of the Everlasting Covenant for my Life. (Now Drink the Cup. Remember you are receiving the Cup from Him. For He said, Drink ye all of it. Matthew 26:27. Therefore, see Him reach out to you).

After this, spend some time praying in the Holy Ghost. Use your prayer language. It is your time to birth the purpose of God in your life. (And you can receive the baptism of the Spirit right now if you're not baptised in the Spirit). Don't rush it, please spend some time praying. This is very important. **You are Free - Spirit, Soul and Body, So Walk in the Fullness of the Covenant Freedom**.

"Now the Lord of peace Himself give you peace always by all means. The Lord be with you all." Amen.

2 Thessalonians 3:16

NOTES

NOTES

CONTACT DETAILS

You have read this book. There are some things that were new to you; others were brought to your attention again. We do believe that you've been blessed. Please use the contact information below, to send us your praise report and more. We will be most honoured to hear from you.

info@wfcci.com or kingghansah@me.com

DG MINISTRIES/WFCC
P O BOX 1221
NEWCASTLE UPON TYNE
NE4 5WA
UK

Visit: DanielGhansah.com or wfcci.com for more information.

ABOUT THE AUTHOR

Rev. Daniel Ghansah is one of the finest men of God you could ever meet. A proven man with Apostolic, Healing and Teaching Anointing. He has great insight into the Word of God; and he expounds the Word of God in a very practical way – making it alive to real life issues thus dealing with spiritual, physical, psychological and social aspects of life.

He is the President and Founder of Word of Faith Church and Daniel Generations. A man of Wisdom and Power. He is the author of **Exploits of Wisdom** which unveils the Wisdom of God; and **Framing Your World – Success in spite of Difficulties.**

Many get stunned as they listen to this great man of God with a ministry backed by signs and wonders.

Rev. D. O. Ghansah is married to a *beautiful lady Irene*, and they are a fruitful couple.

OTHER BOOKS BY THE AUTHOR

> *EXPLOITS OF WISDOM*

> *FRAMING YOUR WORLD – Success in spite of Difficulties*

COMING SOON

- *Cheerful Heart*
- *Accepted, Installed and Restored*
- *The Language of Faith*